Signposts Along
Life's Journey

BIBLE STUDY GUIDE

From the Bible-teaching ministry of

Charles R. Swindoll

INSIGHT FOR LIVING

Chuck graduated in 1963 from Dallas Theological Seminary, where he now serves as the school's fourth president, helping to prepare a new generation of men and women for the ministry. Chuck has served in pastorates in three states: Massachusetts, Texas, and California, including almost twenty-three years at the First Evangelical Free Church in Fullerton, California. His sermon messages have been aired over radio since 1979 as the *Insight for Living* broadcast. A best-selling author, Chuck has written numerous books and booklets on many subjects.

Based on the outlines and transcripts of Chuck's sermons, the study guide text is co-authored by Jason Shepherd, a graduate of the Texas A&M University and Dallas Theological Seminary. He also wrote the Living Insights.

Editor in Chief: Cynthia Swindoll	**Graphics System Administrator:** Bob Haskins
Coauthor of Text: Jason Shepherd	**Director, Communications Division:** John Norton
Senior Editor and Assistant Writer: Wendy Peterson	**Production Coordinator:** Don Bernstein
Copy Editors: Marco Salazar Glenda Schlahta	**Project Coordinator:** Shannon Scharkey
Text Designer: Gary Lett	**Pprinter:** Sinclair Printing Company

Unless otherwise identified, all Scripture references are from the New American Standard Bible, updated edition, copyright © The Lockman Foundation 1960, 1962, 1963, 1968, 1971, 1972, 1973, 1975, 1977, 1995. Used by permission. Scripture taken from the Holy Bible, New International Version © 1973, 1978, 1984 International Bible Society, used by permission of Zondervan Bible Publishers [NIV].

Guide coauthored by Jason Shepherd:
Copyright © 1998 by Charles R. Swindoll, Inc.

Original outlines, charts, and transcripts:
Copyright © 1997 by Charles R. Swindoll, Inc.

An effort has been made to locate sources and obtain permission where necessary for the quotations used in this book. In the event of any unintentional omission, a modification will gladly be incorporated in future printings.

ISBN 1-57972-098-6
STUDY GUIDE COVER DESIGN: Michael Standlee
Printed in the United States of America

CONTENTS

INTRODUCTION

We're all travelers, sojourners on life's road. And it's not always an easy trip. Instead of being drivers in a comfortable car, we sometimes feel more like rafters on a wild river—tossed here and there, at the mercy of the raging torrent. But was life designed to be that way? Are we destined to wander aimlessly as our circumstances dictate our direction and speed?

The Bible answers those questions with a resounding "No!" In fact, it teaches us that the decisions we make have a direct impact on our destination. However, to make good decisions along life's road, we need two invaluable tools: a trustworthy map and accurate signposts. The Bible will be our map in this study guide as it points out six major signposts to look for in the Christian journey. If we trust the map and obey its road signs, we will end up where we want to be—enjoying an intimate relationship with God.

If you feel aimless or almost out of control . . . if you are confused about which road to take . . . or if you just want to be sure that your direction pleases God, this survey of the Christian journey may be just what you need to get—or stay—on track.

So grab your map, and let's hit the road together. Our first significant signpost is just ahead.

Chuck Swindoll

Chuck Swindoll

PUTTING TRUTH
INTO ACTION

K nowledge apart from application falls short of God's desire for
His children. He wants us to apply what we learn so that we
will change and grow. This study guide was prepared with these
goals in mind. As you go through the following pages, we hope your
desire to discover biblical truth will grow as your understanding of
God's Word increases and that you will be encouraged to apply what
you've learned.

To assist you in your study, we've included a section called
Living Insights at the end of each lesson. These exercises will
challenge you to study further and to think of specific ways to put
your discoveries into action.

There are many ways to use this guide—in personal devotions,
group studies, discussions with friends and family, and Sunday school
classes. And, of course, it's an ideal study aid when you're listening
to its corresponding *Insight for Living* radio series.

To benefit most from this study guide, we would encourage you
to consider it a spiritual journal. That's why we've included space
in the Living Insights for recording your thoughts and discoveries.
We hope you'll return to those sections often for review and en-
couragement as you continue to grow in your walk with Christ.

Jason Shepherd
Coauthor of Text
Author of Living Insights

Signposts Along

Life's Journey

Chapter 1

NARROW BRIDGE

Selected Scriptures

There's something intriguing about wayfarers—adventurers who explore exotic lands and encounter hidden cultures. Where do they go? What do they see? What keeps them roaming?

Luckily for us, many of these wanderers have written their stories—from the historian Herodotus, who traveled the Greek and Babylonian empires and preserved the first records of humanity's past, to the American writing legend Louis L'Amour, who chose the life of a hobo, a migratory worker, during the Great Depression. He went from town to town, working for a season or two, then hopping on a train headed for the next job. These travelers have spun their tales from the loom of experience, and we sit at their feet and listen.

What draws us to them, to their journeys, to their discoveries? Henry David Thoreau may very well have pinpointed the reason:

> A traveler is . . . the best symbol of our life. Going from—toward; it is the history of every one of us.[1]

We're all journeyers on this road called life. We don't know what lies around the next bend, what awaits us over the crest of the next hill. Those who are Christians know they'll find something good at the end of their journey. But those who aren't walking with God confidently go their own way, unaware that if they don't walk *with* God on their way *to* God, their journey's end will reach a dreadful place *without* God.

It all depends on the path we take, the signs we follow, the travel guide we use. The only reliable guide for this journey of life

---

1. Henry David Thoreau, as quoted by Bob Moore and Patrick Grauwels, in *Route 66: A Guidebook to the Mother Road* (Del Mar, Calif.: USDC, n.d.), p. 61.

1

is God's Word. The Bible places signs along the side of the road to direct us on our way—some warning of danger ahead; others leading to points of interest and rest. Scripture also starts us on the right path, guiding us to a certain bridge we must cross before we begin our trek toward eternal life.

What is this bridge? You may have seen the sign for it. It's called "Narrow Bridge." And it is the only one that will bring us to God.

The Narrow Bridge

The narrow bridge is none other than Jesus Christ. "No one comes to the Father," Jesus stressed, "but through Me" (John 14:6b). All of Scripture provides signposts that point to Him. Let's look at several from both the Old Testament and the New.

An Old Testament Signpost

Proverbs 14:12, though not directly mentioning Christ, highlights how crucial it is to make sure we're on the right path:

> There is a way which seems right to a man,
> But its end is the way of death.

This sign warns us: Slow Down. Paths that may seem right might actually be wrong, and if we follow them blindly, a wrong choice will end in our death. In the spiritual sense, this means hell, eternal separation from God.

In our multicultural, tolerance-loving society, many ways look right. Buddhism and Hinduism, Islam and New Age are all accorded equal value as paths to eternal life. The one problem, however, is that they exclude Jesus Christ. Some of us might be surprised to learn that Christianity is not the largest belief system in the world. Hindus and secular atheists both outnumber Christians by at least 200 million each.[2] The largest religion remains Islam, with its more than 1.2 billion Muslims. Islam is growing faster than any other faith.[3] The existence of these non-Christian religions reveals, unfortunately, that most of the world follows a way which seems right but will ultimately end in spiritual death.

Other paths that seem right don't exclude Jesus but incorporate

---

2. Patrick Johnstone, *Operation World: The Day-by-Day Guide to Praying for the World*, 5th ed. (Grand Rapids, Mich.: Zondervan Publishing House, 1993), p. 159.

3. Johnstone, *Operation World*, p. 159.

Him into their salvation systems in unbiblical ways. These so-called Christian views either add to or subtract from the true gospel. And many people rightly describe such views as cults. Josh McDowell and Don Stewart define a cult as "a perversion, a distortion of biblical Christianity and/or a rejection of the historic teachings of the Christian church."[4] They also note, "No one is taught in the cults that he can be saved from eternal damnation by simply placing his faith in Jesus Christ."[5]

A cult, for example, may tell you that Jesus was just a good person and that faith in Him is misplaced. Or it may tell you that faith in Christ is not sufficient, that you must also perform some good deeds to achieve salvation. Despite these heresies, many people get lured into cults. Author Bob Larson identifies almost ninety cultic organizations.[6] Their abundance makes it clear that many people are following a way that "seems right"—right into spiritual ruin.

Even some churches, which should be pointing out the narrow bridge and helping others across it, divert people to a wide path of many philosophies that leads them to eternal peril. They proclaim that every human being is a child of God, whether they've been brought into God's family through Christ or not. They ask, "What kind of God would create people and then throw them into hell?" They reassure their listeners that God will save all people in the end. This particular position is known as Universalism, and in many ways its logic seems right. But remember the signpost of Proverbs 14:12—not all ways that seem right at the start will prove to be right in the end.

As we pass from the Old Testament to the New, we find that the warning to "slow down" is much needed. Signposts in the New Testament point us away from different religions, from cults, from philosophies. They direct us away from ways that seem right and point us instead to the only way, the way that is right.

New Testament Signposts

Jesus Himself gave us one of the clearest signposts for salvation in Matthew 7:13–14.

4. Josh McDowell and Don Stewart, *Handbook of Today's Religions* (Nashville, Tenn.: Thomas Nelson Publishers, 1983), p. 17.

5. McDowell and Stewart, *Handbook of Today's Religions,* p. 24.

6. Bob Larson, *Larson's New Book of Cults* (Wheaton, Ill.: Tyndale House Publishers, 1989), table of contents.

> "Enter through the narrow gate; for the gate is wide and the way is broad that leads to destruction, and there are many who enter through it. For the gate is small and the way is narrow that leads to life, and there are few who find it."

Do Jesus' words seem illogical? Humanly speaking, yes. The wide way, or to use our analogy, the wide bridge, seems like a more intelligent choice. If you were behind the wheel, wouldn't you choose a wider bridge? It can accommodate more travelers, and you don't have to steer as carefully. Newer bridges usually have wider lanes too. They're easier to cross and typically a lot safer. Jesus' teaching does contradict human logic; and as a result, most people choose the wide bridge.

Divine wisdom, though, doesn't brake for human logic. God consistently emphasizes the truth of the narrow bridge. Speaking through Peter, God refers to His Son this way:

> "And there is salvation in no one else; for there is no other name under heaven that has been given among men by which we must be saved." (Acts 4:12)

And God's Spirit moved Paul to declare:

> This is good and acceptable in the sight of God our Savior, who desires all men to be saved and to come to the knowledge of the truth. For there is one God, and one mediator also between God and men, the man Christ Jesus. (1 Tim. 2:3–5)

Finally, Jesus Himself left no more room for narrow-versus-wide discussion: "I am *the* way, and *the* truth, and *the* life; no one comes to the Father but through Me" (John 14:6, emphasis added).

Now that you know that crossing the narrow bridge is the only way to reach eternal life, it's time to ask yourself if you've crossed that bridge yet.

Crossing the Narrow Bridge

Hopefully, you have already crossed the narrow bridge to God and put your trust in Jesus Christ. You're now on the road to heaven! But just in case you haven't and you're wondering how to do it, it's really quite simple.

Confess Your Sin

Every bridge exists because a gorge, creek, or some kind of drop-off separates two planes. In the same way, the narrow bridge exists because we are separated from God by our sin. As Isaiah 59:2 says,

> But your iniquities have made a separation
> between you and your God,
> And your sins have hidden His face from you so
> that He does not hear.

That's bad news—and it gets worse. Paul tells us in Romans 6:23 that "the wages of sin is death." In other words, we deserve to be eternally separated from God. We deserve to go to hell.

How do we get out of this mess? By trying to be better people? By trying to build our own bridge of good works? No, we can never be good enough, and besides, God has provided a much more gracious way:

> If we confess our sins, He is faithful and righteous
> to forgive us our sins and to cleanse us from all
> unrighteousness. (1 John 1:9)

God has constructed the bridge for us, at great expense to Himself—it cost Him His Son.

> He made Him who knew no sin to be sin on our
> behalf, so that we might become the righteousness
> of God in Him. (2 Cor. 5:21)

With His own life, Jesus paid the toll for us. All we have to do is confess our sins to God, and He will open the gate of the bridge to us.

Trust in Christ

If you have confessed your sins and let Christ pay the toll, what else must you do to actually cross the bridge into a right relationship with God? You simply need to trust in Jesus Christ. You must believe that His death was the only sacrifice sufficient enough to remove your sin and that His resurrection was the only power strong enough to give you new life.

God knows your heart, and He doesn't require any fancy prayers or rituals to give you salvation. To cross the narrow bridge, simply speak honestly to Him in prayer. Here's a suggestion:

Dear Jesus,
Thank You for dying on the cross for my sins. I believe Your death was meant to bring me salvation. I trust in You as my Savior. Thank You for forgiving my sins and giving me new life. Amen.

If this prayer expresses your desire, you are now on the right road, the only road, to heaven. The Bible promises eternal life to everyone who believes in Christ: "For with the heart a person believes, resulting in righteousness, and with the mouth he confesses, resulting in salvation" (Rom. 10:10).

There's something intriguing about adventurers. Like the great travelers before you, you will have stories of your own to tell. But in the end, it won't matter as much where you've been as where you're going. Are you walking with God? Have you crossed the narrow bridge? Or are you confidently traveling apart from Him? Your direction determines your destination. Choose your path wisely.

 Living Insights

Stephen Covey makes a great point about goal setting for life's travelers. He reminds us to begin the trip with the end in mind: "To begin with the end in mind means to start with a clear understanding of your destination. It means to know where you're going so that you better understand where you are now and so that the steps you take are always in the right direction."[7]

Where are you now? Are your steps taking you in the right direction? Are you making each step deliberately, knowing your goal and how to get there? Or do you find yourself just wandering from path to path? What each path looks like doesn't matter as much as where it leads. What good is it to take the wide bridge when it is merely a ramp to hell? Your decision determines your destination. Will you cross the narrow bridge? Will you trust in Jesus Christ right now? As you think about this invitation, consider the words of Charles Spurgeon.

> Be not like the foolish drunkard who, staggering home one night, saw his candle lit for him. "Two

7. Stephen R. Covey, *The Seven Habits of Highly Effective People: Restoring the Character Ethic* (New York, N.Y.: Simon and Schuster, A Fireside Book, 1989), p. 98.

candles!" said he, for his drunkenness made him see double, "I will blow out one," and as he blew it out, in a moment he was in the dark. Many a person sees double through the drunkenness of sin. He has one life to sow his wild oats in, and then he half expects another in which to turn to God. So, like a fool, he blows out the only candle that he has, and in the dark he will have to lie down forever. Remember, you only have one sun, and after that sets, you will never reach your home. Make haste![8]

"Make haste!" None of us is promised one more day or one more second on this earth. If you haven't crossed the narrow bridge, do it now—while you still have the chance.

8. Charles Spurgeon, *The Quotable Spurgeon* (Wheaton, Ill.: Harold Shaw Publishers, 1990), p. 387.

Chapter 2

DANGEROUS CURVE AHEAD
Romans 6:1–14

Now that we've crossed the "Narrow Bridge," let's continue our journey. What's that signpost up the road? It says "Dangerous Curve Ahead."

"Dangerous"? Well, that's a surprise. With the "Narrow Bridge" in our rearview mirror and a secure eternal destiny beyond the horizon, won't the rest of the journey be a leisurely jaunt? This should be the time to turn on the cruise control, sit back with one hand on the wheel, and soak in some scenery. Right?

Actually, it's just the opposite. When we crossed the "Narrow Bridge," we dragged with us our old, sinful nature. Crossing the bridge changed our destination—we'll go to heaven. It also changed our hearts—we now have a yearning to please God. But crossing the bridge did not unload our fleshly impulses. We still struggle against sin's powerful pull and our old driving habits. With good reason, then, does the Bible warn us about the dangerous curves ahead.

Travelers who are unaware or unconcerned about sin's presence can end up in a ditch, wrecking their witness or stalling out their effectiveness for God.

How can we keep from becoming a casualty? Let's sit beside the apostle Paul and follow his instructions for safe and careful driving.

Road Conditions

In his letter to the Romans, Paul made the nature of the terrain we'll be traveling on our spiritual journey very clear.

First: *All of us were destined to wreck.* Romans 1–3 reveals the depraved nature within every type of traveler—pagans, moralists, and religious people (see especially 3:9–20). Without Christ, without crossing the narrow bridge, all of us were destined to careen off the road and into the gorge of sin separating us from God. We were all sinners and unable to resist our sinful urges. We were slaves to those desires.

Second: *Christ removed sin's grasp from the steering wheel.* Chapter 3 does not end in despair. Jesus atoned for our sins, and His redemption has freed us from sin's mastery and has given us His righteousness (vv. 21–26). We are now justified in God's sight and have the opportunity to experience spiritual freedom[1] (see also Luke 4:18; John 8:32, 36; Rom. 6:7; 8:2, 31–32; Gal. 5:1, 13; 1 Pet. 2:16).

Third: *Many Christians still succumb to sin's backseat driving.* Tragically, many of us behave as if sin were still in control, despite our newfound freedom. That old nature still wants to drive where it pleases. It entices us off the straight and narrow road and onto the dead-end path of sinful pleasure. And it's a struggle to tune it out and heed our new nature, as Paul wrote so honestly:

> For what I am doing, I do not understand; for I am not practicing what I would like to do, but I am doing the very thing I hate. (Rom. 7:15; see also v. 19)

We're redeemed, we're justified, we're set free—yet we seem resigned to the myth that sin has the upper hand. Why? Perhaps we presume too much on God's gracious forgiveness in 1 John 1:9 instead of taking the responsibility of heeding the signpost of Romans 6.

Negotiating the Dangerous Curve: Romans 6

Romans 6 prepares us for the "Dangerous Curve Ahead." It warns us all to watch the road ahead and get ready to do some deft driving. To those about to run off the road, Paul stands up and holds out a halting hand:

> What shall we say then? Are we to continue in sin so that grace may increase? May it never be! How shall we who died to sin still live in it? (vv. 1–2)

The very thought of abusing grace with sinful indulgence horrifies the apostle. So Paul's whole point in Romans 6 is that the power of the old sinful nature that once controlled us has been revoked—nullified. What we must learn now is how to keep it out of the driver's seat. From Paul's words in the first half of this chapter, we can glean three action steps to do just that—know, consider, and present.

Know

Let's begin with what we are to *know.*

---

1. Justification is the sovereign act of God whereby He declares righteous the believing sinner while we're still in a sinning state.

Or do you not know that all of us who have been baptized into Christ Jesus have been baptized into His death? Therefore we have been buried with Him through baptism into death, so that as Christ was raised from the dead through the glory of the Father, so we too might walk in newness of life. For if we have become united with Him in the likeness of His death, certainly we shall also be in the likeness of His resurrection, knowing this, that our old self was crucified with Him, in order that our body of sin might be done away with, so that we would no longer be slaves to sin; for he who has died is freed from sin.

Now if we have died with Christ, we believe that we shall also live with Him, knowing that Christ, having been raised from the dead, is never to die again; death no longer is master over Him. For the death that He died, He died to sin once for all; but the life that He lives, He lives to God. (vv. 3–10)

The word *baptized*, *baptizō* in Greek, comes from the root *baptō*, a term used in the first century for dipping a garment first into bleach and then into dye, cleansing and changing the color of the cloth. As J. Dwight Pentecost explains,

The word metaphorically meant to change identity, to change appearance, or even to change relationships.

To the Jewish mind, *baptizō* had in it both the idea of cleansing and consecration to a new identity or a new relationship.[2]

When Christ died on the cross, He was dipped or baptized into death (see Luke 12:50). He rose from the grave, and His perishable body changed to an imperishable one (see 1 Cor. 15:42–49; 1 John 3:2). When we trust in Him for eternal life, we become dipped into His death and resurrection. Similarly, our identity changes (see 2 Cor. 5:17). We don't see or hear it; we may not even feel it. But it changes nevertheless. Jesus' death to sin becomes our death to sin; His new life becomes our new life. Positionally, our

2. See J. Dwight Pentecost, *The Words and Works of Jesus Christ: A Study in the Life of Christ* (Grand Rapids, Mich.: Zondervan Publishing House, Academie Books, 1981), p. 83.

old nature dies on the cross, and with it, its dominion over us (see Col. 2:12–15).

This doesn't mean we are free from the reality of sin's presence in our old nature, but its mastery and domination over us is null and void. We now have the power to choose not to sin, and a victorious walk begins with knowing this fact.

Consider

Once we *know*, there is something we need to *consider.*

> Even so consider yourselves to be dead to sin, but alive to God in Christ Jesus. (Rom. 6:11)

To experience the freedom Christ has given us, we must transform our way of thinking (see 12:2). We must consider it to be true that, since we died with Christ, we are dead to sin's rule over our lives; and since we were raised with Christ, we are alive to God's power. "Therefore," Paul says,

> do not let sin reign in your mortal body so that you obey its lusts. (6:12)

Because we're human, we'll never be sinless. But we can become more and more aware of our choice to avoid sin and become stronger at resisting it.

Present

Knowing the truth of our freedom and counting it as real brings us to our third crucial action step: *present.*

> And do not go on presenting the members of your body to sin as instruments of unrighteousness; but present yourselves to God as those alive from the dead, and your members as instruments of righteousness to God. For sin shall not be master over you, for you are not under law but under grace. (vv. 13–14)

Christ redeemed our bodies as well as our souls. With His blood He purchased all our members—our hands, feet, arms, legs, eyes, ears . . . everything. And He has set them apart and empowered them for His glory. "So," Paul says, "stop giving them to evil! Offer them to God as instruments of good."

Conclusion

Are you surprised that the Christian life is such a struggle? Surprised that you'll actually have to use a strategy to live a God-pleasing life? A cursory examination of Jesus' life is enough to show us that we should be anything but surprised. Of all the ways He could have come to earth, He chose the way of struggle. He took upon himself a human body and fought every impulse: hunger, anger, betrayal, and all the rest. And He Himself warned us that His way would not be easy:

> "For the gate is small and the way is narrow that leads to life, and there are few who find it." (Matt. 7:14)

Why should we expect our lives to be any different from His? Let's not be surprised when sin tempts us. And let's be prepared to defeat it.

 Living Insights

Texans have a knack for making something good out of what's really bad. Take roadkill, for example. Some of the finer novelty shops in Texas stock a product called "Pure Texas Armadillo: Sun-dried and Road-tenderized." The label on the can lists these ingredients: "Pure sun-dried armadillo run over by a log truck three miles south of Pollok, Texas. Not over 20 percent hair, gravel, and foreign matter."

Roadkill, though, is no laughing matter when *you're* the one caught in the headlights, about to be run over.

We can quickly become victims if we carelessly wander into sin's path, not realizing the danger in front of us. To avoid becoming spiritual roadkill, let's heed the warning sign we examined in Romans 6. Let's start by developing a personalized strategy based on the three action steps *know*, *consider*, and *present*.

Take a few minutes to consider what the Bible says about you. After each reference, write out a short statement starting with, "I know I am . . ."

John 1:12 _____

_____

John 8:36 _____

12

John 15:15 _____

_____

1 Corinthians 3:16 _____

_____

Ephesians 2:10_____

_____

Colossians 2:10 _____

_____

Look back at this list, and allow all of that new knowledge to soak in. Now remind yourself that you not only need to know these truths, but you also need to consider them as reality. They're not just theories that someday may come true. They're true right now; they're true of you.

Finally, write out some specific ways you will present yourself to God in light of this knowledge. How will you act differently? What kind of choices will you make based on your new perspective?

_____

_____

_____

_____

_____

Chapter 3
ROADSIDE PARK
Hebrews 4:1–11

Americans live life in the fast lane. From soccer moms to work-aholics, we all contribute to the fast-paced lifestyle that characterizes our culture. Unfortunately, the busy atmosphere we have created has caused a lot of anxiety. Two of the most popular prescription drugs in America are Prozac, used to treat depression, and Tagamet, which eases pain caused by ulcers.

Unfortunately, our Christian faith often contributes to our anxiety instead of soothing it. With the pure motive of wanting to participate in God's plan, we can overcommit to church activities. As a result, our faith becomes one more arena in which we do as much as possible, as fast as possible.

Sometimes our motives are not so pure. We overinvolve ourselves because we want God to be happy with us. We feel that if we don't do our share at the church, God will be displeased. As a result, we fall into a works mentality that undermines the gospel of liberty.

As we travel down this "fast lane," we could sure use something like a "roadside park." There's nothing quite like the sight of a sign announcing, "Rest Area Ahead." It's always a relief to pull off the road, stretch our legs, find some shade, and have a cold drink.

As we struggle to survive in our rush-hour world, God offers us rest, a spiritual "roadside park." So let's take advantage of it. Let's pull out of the fast lane for awhile and into the parking space God has reserved for us. There we can refuel and refresh ourselves, away from the grind of everyday life.

The Exit Ramp to the Roadside Park

Hebrews 4:1–11 hints at the kind of rest we're after. The passage primarily refers to eternal rest, teaching that, through faith in Jesus Christ, we can have the assurance of entering the rest of the Lord when we go to heaven.

But we can also have rest right now. We don't have to wait for heaven to find relief. We can live today in the hope and reality of our eternal future, learning to practice a Sabbath in the here and now that gives us a taste of our ultimate Sabbath—heaven.

Israel's Rest Spurned

An effective method of learning is to consider the failures of those who have gone before you. In the latter part of Hebrews 3, the author cites the example of the Israelites, who failed to enter into the Lord's rest. Here's what Hebrews says about them:

> Who were they who heard and rebelled? Were they not all those Moses led out of Egypt? And with whom was he angry for forty years? Was it not with those who sinned, whose bodies fell in the desert? And to whom did God swear that they would never enter his rest if not to those who disobeyed? So we see that they were not able to enter, because of their unbelief. (vv. 16–19 NIV)

That wilderness landscape is not a picture you'd want to hang over your sofa. True, in the background, just over the horizon, there's a land flowing with milk and honey—a really big roadside park. But in the foreground lie the bloated corpses of the unfaithful—spiritual roadkill. The vultures circle overhead in descending spirals, and the blazing sun glares down with its unrelenting and unsympathetic stare.

What a tragedy! And one the author to the Hebrews hopes we won't relive in our own lives.

God's Rest Offered

It's against the background of this graphic picture of the consequences of unbelief that the writer issues his warning in 4:1.

The Warning

> Therefore, since the promise of entering his rest still stands, let us be careful that none of you be found to have fallen short of it. (NIV)

The Israelites were so close to entering the Promised Land. They stood on the very banks of the Jordan with their toes in the water and gazed upon the shade offered on its other bank. But despite the relentless life they lived as nomads, despite the sight of a new home across the river, they failed to enter into the rest the Lord had prepared for them. They became filled with fear of the giants in Canaan rather than trusting in their awesome God; and as a result, they failed to cross the river. Instead, they sealed their doom to become dust for the desert.

Just as the land of promise stretched before the Israelites, so God's rest beckons us from the side of the road. But entering it is not automatic.

Before we can enter into God's rest, we have to understand what it is. So let's define what we mean by "rest." When the Lord rested on the seventh day of Creation, He called that day the Sabbath (see Exod. 20:11). *Sabbath* comes from the Hebrew root *shabath*, which means "to cease, desist, rest."

Many of us regard Sunday as our Sabbath; but while church might be a place of rest for some, others know it as a place of hard work and heavy responsibility. So rather than limiting our idea of Sabbath-rest to one day, let's view it as a time in which we cease from activity and busyness. This could be Sunday or another day— or it might be just an hour or two or a whole weekend. Whenever we do it, we should rest and remember the Lord at that time.

The Explanation

Hebrews 4:2–8 provides us with three aids for entering into God's rest: faith, ceasing, and time.

Rest requires faith.

> For we also have had the gospel preached to us, just as they did; but the message they heard was of no value to them, because those who heard did not combine it with faith. Now we who have believed enter that rest, just as God has said,
> "So I declared on oath in my anger,
>   'They shall never enter my rest.'"
> And yet his work has been finished since the creation of the world. (vv. 2–3 NIV)

Couched within these two verses is a simple truth: Hearing without believing is worthless. The Israelites heard but did not believe, and the good news "was of no value to them." Likewise, if we fail to believe in God's care and provision for us, we, too, will have no rest. We have to believe that God will provide for us if we choose, for example, not to work on Saturdays. We have to believe that honoring God is more important than making extra money or buying more creature comforts for our homes. And certainly God does not require us to be overinvolved in church activities. We won't win a special place in His heart by trying to contribute to our salvation with a busy schedule.

Rest requires ceasing.

> For somewhere he has spoken about the seventh day in these words: "And on the seventh day God rested from all his work." And again in the passage above he says, "They shall never enter my rest."
> It still remains that some will enter that rest, and those who formerly had the gospel preached to them did not go in, because of their disobedience. (vv. 4–6 NIV)

In this section the writer goes all the way back to the Creation account, quoting from Genesis 2:2. God Himself established the pattern of rest when He worked six days and rested on the seventh. The first six days of Creation are marked off by the phrase "evening and . . . morning" (Gen. 1:5, 8, 13, 19, 23, 31). However, when we come to the seventh day, no "evening and . . . morning" marks off time boundaries (2:1–3). And work is not mentioned on subsequent days. Meaning what? Meaning that His rest from Creation continues—He left the gate open to those green pastures of His rest for all who not only place their faith for salvation in Him but who live their daily lives by faith.

Does your faith show itself in your ability to stop and rest in God? Do you have a day in which time doesn't matter? Or are you still on the other side of the Jordan, pacing back and forth and biting your nails over all the errands and chores, spiritual or otherwise, that have yet to be done?

Rest requires time.

> Therefore God again set a certain day, calling it Today, when a long time later he spoke through David, as was said before:
> "Today, if you hear his voice,
>   do not harden your hearts."
> For if Joshua had given them rest, God would not have spoken later about another day. (vv. 7–8 NIV)

Twice in these verses the writer stresses the urgency of entering into God's rest with the word *today. Now* is the time! Unfortunately, we tend to front-load our schedules with urgent items that take over our "now" and push entering God's rest to "later." We need to remember Jesus' words to a hurried world:

> "Come to Me, all who are weary and heavy-laden, and I will give you rest. Take My yoke upon you and learn from Me, for I am gentle and humble in heart, and you will find rest for your souls. For My yoke is easy and My burden is light." (Matt. 11:28–30)

The Command

Since entering God's rest isn't automatic, the writer next issues a strong command.

> Let us, therefore, make every effort to enter that rest, so that no one will fall by following their example of disobedience. (Heb. 4:11 NIV)

Why "make every effort"? Why do we need to work so hard at resting, of all things? Because old habits are hard to break. And beyond that, our ability to rest now testifies to our belief in God's promise of future rest. Our lifestyle reflects our faith. What does your pace show about what you believe?

Our Rest Provided

Do you see the signpost now? "Roadside Park, Next Right." Go ahead and take the exit. Ease your foot off the accelerator and loosen the vise grip you have on the steering wheel. Take advantage of the opportunity God has provided. It's there, just waiting for you.

 Living Insights

It would be strange to "do" something after a lesson on resting. So here are a few things to *stop* doing. Beside each reference, write out the basic application.

Stop Worrying

Luke 12:22–34 _____

_____

_____

18

Philippians 4:6–7 _____

_____
_____

Stop Churning
Exodus 20:8–11_____

_____
_____

Psalm 37:8–9_____

_____
_____

Mark 6:31–32 _____

_____
_____

Stop Procrastinating
Joshua 18:3 _____

_____
_____

Joshua asked a great question in 18:3. How long will we wait to take advantage of the wonderful rest God offers? Although we will experience the ultimate rest in heaven, a taste of it awaits us right now. Let's not wait any longer to enjoy it.

Chapter 4
DRIVE FRIENDLY
Romans 14:1–18

Texas is "The Friendly State." In the days when they used to print state mottoes on license plates, you could see that phrase clearly imprinted along the bottom of each distinctive black-on-white plate. The state's name itself comes from a Hasinai Indian term, *tejas*, meaning "friends."

In the spirit of the state's slogan, the Texas Department of Public Safety has instituted its own motto: "Drive Friendly." In short, they want travelers to exhibit state spirit by being kind to one another on the road. As Texans and visitors alike enter the state from every conceivable direction, they pass the unmistakable triangular road signs imploring them with this simple request. In the state's interior, too, just about every interstate, freeway, and bypass boasts at least one "Drive Friendly" sign.

Any experienced motorist could tell you what the Department of Safety had in mind when it created the slogan. Specifically, they wanted travelers to live peacefully with one another despite their many different traveling styles. For example, some might want to travel at the state-mandated speed limit of seventy-five miles per hour. Others may not feel comfortable going that fast, preferring fifty-five instead.

Unfortunately, the two groups—the "speedsters" and the "slowpokes"—don't get along very well on the highway. The speedsters want to go full speed ahead, all that the law allows. And sometimes they'll flash their lights, honk their horn, shake their fist and curse, tailgate, or swerve around anyone who dares to slow them down. They hold slowpokes in contempt, griping, "People like that need to get off the road. They're causing pileups!"

The slowpokes, on the other hand, don't feel comfortable going as fast. They are convinced that the others are driving recklessly, putting everyone in danger. Sometimes, when they feel that traffic is moving too fast, they'll try to cut off those speedy drivers and slow them down. Slowpokes may even judge those going full speed with accusations like, "That guy's driving way too fast! Is he trying to get us all killed?"

The Christian life also has its "speedsters" and "slowpokes." The

20

speedsters are those who take advantage of the full range of freedom Christ has given us, but sometimes they do so to the point of being insensitive or reckless with the well-being of others. And the slow-pokes are those who sometimes try to impose their own limitations on other drivers. They may try to weigh others down with their personal convictions.

How do we get these two groups to "drive friendly"? Should the "speedsters" simply give up their freedom in order to keep the peace? Or should they blow off the concerns of the slowpokes because they're weaker in the faith? The apostle Paul would respond with a resounding "No!" to both questions.

No Heavy Loads Beyond This Point

Many of us, unfortunately, give up our freedom too quickly. We may begin to feel that good Christians take stands on "important" issues, and the more sanctified we are, the more stands we take. In that kind of thinking, a strong Christian abstains from movies and television, has half an hour of quiet time every day, and can clearly articulate the "proper" positions on Sabbath rest, alcohol, and dancing, just to mention a few. When we take on a load like this, however, we wind up stalling out under the weight of borrowed beliefs. Or worse, we begin to load others down with a long list of burdensome restrictions.

Paul knew the destination of weaker believers who traveled down this road. In fact, one of his flocks had already arrived there. They were the Galatians, and they had fallen into legalism.

> You foolish Galatians, who has bewitched you, before whose eyes Jesus Christ was publicly portrayed as crucified? This is the only thing I want to find out from you: did you receive the Spirit by the works of the Law, or by hearing with faith? Are you so foolish? Having begun by the Spirit, are you now being perfected by the flesh? (Gal. 3:1–3)

These are harsh words from a confused and angry spiritual father. But they are appropriate. The Galatians had been influenced by a group of people known as Judaizers. The Judaizers had convinced them that faith in Christ was not enough—they needed to fulfill the requirements of Jewish Law in order to be saved. And the Galatian Christians bought right into their convictions.

Paul's response was blunt and to the point. He wanted to know how they could possibly think they could begin the Christian life in one way, by the Spirit; and then move on toward maturity in another, by the flesh. For Paul, such a notion was absolutely ludicrous. Later in the letter he emphasized his point again:

> It was for freedom that Christ set us free; therefore keep standing firm and do not be subject again to a yoke of slavery. (5:1)

"It was for freedom that Christ set us free." What a phenomenal truth! Christ has freed us from:

- the power and guilt of sin
- God's wrath
- the tyranny of Satan and his demons
- the curse of the Law
- the fear of judgment
- an accusing conscience
- others' expectations

If Christ Himself has set us free, then we should hold on to our freedom and not give it up too easily. We should not allow ourselves or our weaker brothers and sisters to adopt a works mentality. Because when we give in to legalism, we are really seeking to please people—but when we live by grace, we seek to please God.

So we should encourage each other toward freedom in Christ. We must "keep standing firm" in our freedom and for the freedom of others. We must live by grace and allow ourselves and others to receive from the Lord a personal set of convictions. No heavy loads beyond this point.

Does this mean that we are free from all standards? Of course not. We should not use Christ's freedom as a license for sin. God has created us in "Christ Jesus for good works" (Eph. 2:10)—He wants all His people to be passionate about serving Him. So if speedsters shrug off convictions so that their consciences won't bother them as they sin, they have veered off course just as much as the slowpokes who become legalists.

Four Signposts for Friendly Driving

In Romans 14, Paul goes into even greater detail regarding the issue of personal freedom, setting forth four practical principles to help us release others in grace. The first signpost is found in verses 1–4.

Signpost One: Accept Others

> Now accept the one who is weak in faith, but not for the purpose of passing judgment on his opinions. One person has faith that he may eat all things, but he who is weak eats vegetables only. The one who eats is not to regard with contempt the one who does not eat, and the one who does not eat is not to judge the one who eats, for God has accepted him. Who are you to judge the servant of another? To his own master he stands or falls; and he will stand, for the Lord is able to make him stand.

The problem Paul was addressing in Romans 14 was not a food problem. It was a love problem, an *acceptance* problem. It still is. How often do we restrict our love by making it conditional? How often does our acceptance depend on how others measure up to our own set of expectations?

Whether it's the meat sacrificed in a heathen temple or the new film showing in the movie theater, the principle is the same: *Accept one another, because that is basic to cultivating freedom.*

Paul points out that, when we don't accept one another, we generally respond in two rejecting ways. He mentions the first in verse 3a: "The one who eats is not to regard with *contempt* the one who does not eat" (emphasis added). This is the speedster—the one who feels the freedom to do all things. Speedsters tend to look at "slower" believers and view them with *contempt*, a word that means to "despise."[1]

Paul mentions the second form of rejection in verse 3b: "The one who does not eat is not to *judge* the one who eats" (emphasis added). This is the slowpoke—the one who has developed a definite stance on several issues. Sometimes the background of these weaker

1. Sakae Kubo, *A Reader's Greek-English Lexicon of the New Testament and a Beginner's Guide for the Translation of New Testament Greek*, Andrews University Monographs, vol. 4 (Berrien Springs, Mich.: Andrews University Press; Grand Rapids, Mich.: Zondervan Publishing House, Academic and Professional Books, 1975), p. 145.

believers makes them sensitive to these particular areas, much like the Roman believers whose pagan backgrounds turned them off to meat offered to idols. Some weaker believers may come from life-styles that cause them to be repulsed by drinking, dancing, and other activities. Slowpokes can tend to *judge* believers who don't understand and adopt their views, which means they may "pass an unfavorable judgment upon, criticise, find fault with, condemn."[2]

No matter how strongly we may feel about a certain issue, no matter what the devastation we have seen as a result of some behaviors, judging another who disagrees with us or looking down our nose with contempt is wrong. Instead, we need to respond in the spirit of acceptance. We need to "drive friendly."

Why? Because, as Paul explains in verse 4, another person's convictions are none of our business. Do we know better than God? Who are we to pass a verdict on other people's lifestyles? It's God's job to direct them. It's our job to trust Him and accept them.

Acceptance encourages spiritual freedom, and freedom allows others to be themselves. Consider the next four verses of Romans 14 as we approach the second signpost.

Signpost Two: Let Others Decide for Themselves

> One person regards one day above another, an-other regards every day alike. Each person must be fully convinced in his own mind. He who observes the day, observes it for the Lord, and he who eats, does so for the Lord, for he gives thanks to God; and he who eats not, for the Lord he does not eat, and gives thanks to God. For not one of us lives for himself, and not one dies for himself; for if we live, we live for the Lord, or if we die, we die for the Lord; therefore whether we live or die, we are the Lord's. (vv. 5–8)

Do you want to help others grow to maturity? Here's how. Let them grow up differently. Let them unfold to blossom at their own pace and in their own way. Let them decide for themselves. Let them have the freedom to fail and learn from their own mistakes.

2. Walter Bauer, *A Greek-English Lexicon of the New Testament and Other Early Christian Literature*, 2d ed. Revised and augmented by F. Wilbur Gingrich and Frederick W. Danker, from Walter Bauer's 5th ed., 1958 (Chicago, Ill.: University of Chicago Press, 1979), p. 452.

Paul's words in verses 5–8 point to our second crucial principle: *Refusing to dictate to others allows the Lord freedom to direct their lives.*

The slowpokes tend to struggle against this hands-off approach. They believe so firmly in their convictions that they can't conceive how anyone could practice the Christian life without them. Their desire to convince others of the evil effects of certain liberties may cause them to push their personal convictions into community standards.

Speedsters also struggle with letting others grow at their own pace. They think the slowpokes need to just calm down. But forcing a weaker believer to grow up too fast can have a devastating effect as well.

So Paul stresses that each of us belongs to the Lord. When we realize that truth, we will stop dictating and start trusting each other to glorify God in our own way, and we'll start trusting the Lord to direct the steps of each of His children.

Signpost Three: Refuse to Judge Others

Paul provides the third signpost in verses 9–12.

> For to this end Christ died and lived again, that He might be Lord both of the dead and of the living.
>
> But you, why do you judge your brother? Or you again, why do you regard your brother with contempt? For we will all stand before the judgment seat of God. For it is written,
>
> "As I live, says the Lord, every knee shall bow to Me,
> And every tongue shall give praise to God."
> So then each one of us will give an account of himself to God.

If there's one thing this passage makes clear, it is this: there is only One who is qualified to judge—God. What qualifies Him and disqualifies us? He is omniscient, knowing all the facts. We are not. He can see into people's hearts, reading motives. We cannot. He is infinite, having "the big picture." We are not and do not. Having poor spiritual eyesight, we live with blind spots and blurred perspectives. Our very humanness guarantees that we are imperfect, inconsistent, and subjective. Not to mention hurtful. In a chapter titled "Judgment Is Destructive" in his book *Guilt and Grace*, counselor Paul Tournier described the harm we do when we judge each other.

In all fields, even those of culture and art, other people's judgment exercises a paralysing effect. Fear of criticism kills spontaneity; it prevents men from showing themselves and expressing themselves freely, as they are. Much courage is needed to paint a picture, to write a book, to erect a building designed along new architectural lines, or to formulate an independent opinion or an original idea. . . .

. . . My wife said recently, "At bottom, we must always ask ourselves, not whether what we say to someone is well-founded or not, but whether it is constructive or destructive for him."[3]

Our third principle, then, is this: *Freeing others means we never assume a position we're not qualified to fill.* Does this mean that we never confront sin or speak truthfully to someone who is straying into false beliefs? Certainly not. But it does mean that we scrutinize our own motives so we don't correct others out of self-righteousness or our desire to control. It means we do it out of love, with their best interests at heart (see Matt. 7:1–5; Gal. 6:1). It also means that we should not demean weaker believers because of their weakness. They are valuable to the Lord, and He desires them to grow and mature—with our help (see Rom. 14:19–21; 15:1–2, 7).

Ultimately, we will please God only when we seek to glorify Jesus Christ and live for Him alone. When we do that, we will live more peacefully with each other, because we're not trying to sit in the Driver's seat.

Signpost Four: Express Your Liberty Wisely

The final signpost flows out of Romans 14:13–18.

Therefore let us not judge one another anymore, but rather determine this—not to put an obstacle or a stumbling block in a brother's way. I know and am convinced in the Lord Jesus that nothing is unclean in itself; but to him who thinks anything to be unclean, to him it is unclean. For if because of food your brother is hurt, you are no longer walking according to love. Do not destroy with your food

---

3. Paul Tournier, *Guilt and Grace: A Psychological Study*, trans. Arthur W. Heathcote, J. J. Henry, and P. J. Allcock (San Francisco, Calif.: Harper and Row, Publishers, 1962), pp. 98–99.

him for whom Christ died. Therefore do not let what is for you a good thing be spoken of as evil; for the kingdom of God is not eating and drinking, but righteousness and peace and joy in the Holy Spirit. For he who in this way serves Christ is acceptable to God and approved by men.

Essentially, Paul is saying that we must restrain our liberty for the sake of other believers. Love must rule our actions, just as it ruled our Lord's. His love moved Him to buy us with His blood. Our principle, therefore, is this: *Loving others requires us to express our liberty wisely.*

How can we do this? By enjoying our liberty without flaunting it . . . quietly, privately, and with those of like mind who aren't offended by the liberty. And by being willing to open our hearts and allow love to limit our liberty.[4]

Driving friendly isn't an easy thing to do. It takes control and constantly reminds us that we're all headed in the same direction. We all want to glorify God with our lives. As we travel together, we need to remember to live freely by grace. We need to remember the four signposts as we seek to honor God with our lives.

 Living Insights

Consider the following scenarios. Imagine how the situation would play out in your world with the people in your life. After creating the scene in your mind, respond to the follow-up questions.

Case #1

Your teenage daughter's date arrives at the door. He seems like a good boy, and you feel confident that he'll treat your little girl with respect and courtesy. When she comes out to greet him, she's wearing too much makeup and an outfit that reveals a little too much. She doesn't look anything like a streetwalker, but it's not a look you prefer. You're thrown off balance because she's always proven herself trustworthy. Then the really big news comes: They want to go dancing at a club.

---

4. See Timothy S. Warren (class notes for Biblical Communication, Dallas Theological Seminary, 1989; revised 1994), p. 125.

What would your natural response be? _____

_____

_____

Which of the four signposts should you consider before taking
action? _____

_____

_____

Based on those considerations, how would you respond in order
to model grace to your daughter and her date without compromising
your convictions?_____

_____

_____

_____

_____

Case #2

Your six-year-old boy comes home from school talking about
the sixth *Jurassic Park* sequel that opens tonight. His best friend's
mom is organizing a group trip to the movie theater, and she's going
to be calling to invite him. You've read the reviews, and this latest
installment is more graphic and violent than all the others com-
bined, and you know it will be too much for your son. There's no
choice; you'll have to decline the invitation. But what are you going
to say to the other mom?

What would be your natural response? _____

_____

Which signpost should you consider before acting? _____

_____

_____

_____

Based on those considerations, how would you model Romans 14 to this woman?_____

_____

_____

_____

_____

Case #3

One of your favorite programs at church is the "Dinner Fellowship" groups in which you're assigned to a different group each semester. Each member takes a turn hosting a dinner party, and your turn is tonight. You've spent all week shopping for the freshest ingredients, and the last two days have been a frenzy of food preparation. You're having Cornish hens glazed with orange marmalade and stuffed with wild rice. Each side dish, bread, and dessert has been selected to perfectly complement the Cornish hens. And the wine—you spent hours combing through books and magazine articles to find just the right beverage for the occasion. It's chilling in the refrigerator with only minutes to go before the guests arrive.

Then the phone rings. It's Bill, one of the members of the group, and he has invited a friend. The friend is a new Christian and comes from a background of heavy drinking. Bill was just calling to make sure there won't be any alcohol at the dinner.

What would be your natural response? _____

_____

Which signpost should you consider? _____

_____

Based on that principle, what would you do? _____

_____

_____

_____

_____

29

Chapter 5

CAUTION: RAILROAD CROSSING

1 Samuel 18–20; 2 Timothy 4:9–18

J ust one more light," you say to yourself as you're trying to deliver your pile of slacks, shirts, and blouses to the dry cleaners. They close in five minutes, and your last set of pressed clothes is hanging in the closet. If you don't get the garments to the cleaners tonight, you'll have nothing to wear for the next few days. You make it to that last traffic light, and the cleaners is just a block away. It looks like you're going to make it. Then one of the motorist's worst nightmares comes true. Large candy-striped guard rails descend from the sky. Red lights flash on and off, and a loud alarm begins ringing. A train is coming, and you're faced with a very aggravating inconvenience.

None of us likes to be hindered on our way. It's frustrating, anxiety-producing, and just plain unpleasant. Trains stop us now and then, but most of our hindrances come from people—people who bring conflict and opposition into our lives, people whose difficult behavior brings the guard rails down and our guard up. As we seek to grow in our spiritual lives, that opposition often comes from an unlikely source—fellow Christians. Eugene Peterson explains.

> When people become Christians, they don't at the same moment become nice. This always comes as something of a surprise. Conversion to Christ and his ways doesn't automatically furnish a person with impeccable manners and suitable morals. . . .
>
> When Christian believers gather in churches, everything that can go wrong sooner or later does. . . .
>
> So Christian churches are not, as a rule, model communities of good behavior.[1]

How can we deal with the hurtful, even antagonistic, people

1. Eugene H. Peterson, *The Message: The New Testament in Contemporary English* (Colorado Springs, Colo.: NavPress, 1993), pp. 337, 478.

who will inevitably come our way? We need to prepare ourselves to encounter opposition from people within our churches, Bible studies, and fellowship groups. So let's take a lesson from two old, battle-scarred pros: David the fugitive and Paul the prisoner.

David

In the Bible-story memories we carry from childhood, David's triumphant encounter with Goliath stands out as the high point of his life. We remember him going from victory to victory, sailing serenely along on his cruise from shepherd to king.

Scripture, however, tells a very different story. The slaying of the profane giant may have been David's most notable achievement up to that time, but it certainly didn't launch him onto smooth seas. Rather, he was cast adrift on a tumultuous ocean of drenching waves and perilous winds. And he had to navigate that course for many years.[2]

Instant Fame

David's troubles began, ironically, in the midst of his successes. After slaying Goliath and inspiring his fellow Israelites to rout the arrogant Philistines, David was made a commander of the army by a grateful King Saul (1 Sam. 17:45–18:5). The people delighted in his success and cheered his leap from society's lowest rung to its highest. The women even composed a song to praise him:

"Saul has slain his thousands,
And David his ten thousands." (1 Sam. 18:7b)

Unlike many celebrities today, David handled his stellar success admirably. Verse 30 says, "David behaved himself more wisely than all the servants of Saul." Instead of wearing his fame like a cheap fad, he clothed himself with class and dignity.

The Opposition of Saul

Although David handled himself with humility, his rising star still ignited King Saul's smoldering paranoia. The women's song of praise, certainly not meant to demean Saul, set him off like a powder

---

2. Adapted from "Aftermath of a Giant-Killing," in the study guide *David: A Man of Passion and Destiny*, coauthored by Bryce Klabunde, from the Bible-teaching ministry of Charles R. Swindoll (Anaheim, Calif.: Insight for Living, 1997), p. 35.

keg. The comparison of "thousands" and "ten thousands" was never meant to imply that David was ten times better than Saul, but that's how Saul took it.

> Then Saul became very angry, for this saying displeased him; and he said, "They have ascribed to David ten thousands, but to me they have ascribed thousands. Now what more can he have but the kingdom?" (18:8)

And with that, the chase was on. Saul's reaction was like a runaway train in David's life. Just a few verses later, Saul is steaming down at David full-bore, hurling spears at him (18:11; 19:10). Sadly, Saul's jealousy, paranoia, and madness started an obsessive pursuit that lasted for more than a dozen years. From that time until Saul's death, David would be a fugitive, hiding in caves in the wilderness and scrabbling to survive.

David faced a jealous king who wanted to protect his throne and his ego. But he wasn't the only man of God who faced opposition.

Paul

The Apostle Paul wrote his second letter to Timothy while deep in the belly of a citadel. All sound was smothered and all sunlight snuffed out by the tons of dank mortar surrounding his dungeon cell. Down narrow stairwells and beyond vaulted cellars, a flickering torch provided enough light for Paul to etch out his final words to one of his closest disciples. This was more than just another prison cell. Paul was nearing the end of his life, and he knew it.

He wrote the letter after returning from the Roman court's *prima actio*, or "first hearing."[3] This hearing was an opportunity for Paul's friends to step forward and testify to his character and refute the Roman emperor's charge that Paul was a traitor.[4] But Paul's friends never showed up. He wrote, "At my first defense no one supported me, but all deserted me" (4:16). He stood alone before the court, and alone he returned to his dark hole.

3. Ralph Earle, "2 Timothy," in *The Expositor's Bible Commentary*, gen. ed. Frank E. Gaebelein (Grand Rapids, Mich.: Zondervan Publishing House, Regency Reference Library, 1978), vol. 11, p. 416.

4. A. Duane Litfin, "2 Timothy," in *The Bible Knowledge Commentary*, New Testament edition, ed. John F. Walvoord and Roy B. Zuck (Wheaton, Ill.: Scripture Press Publications, Victor Books, 1983), p. 759.

This was the setting in which Paul wrote his final epistle. In the tradition of a Jewish "testament," in which a dying leader imparts his final wisdom to his followers,[5] Paul gave solid instructions to Timothy and also made honest mention of two men who opposed his ministry—one by deserting him, and the other by attacking him.

Demas

Paul implored Timothy, "Make every effort to come to me soon; for Demas, having loved this present world, has deserted me and gone to Thessalonica" (2 Tim. 4:9–10).

Others had forsaken Paul before (v. 16), but here he named Demas in particular. Demas represents one extreme in the spectrum of opposition. His method was passive—he simply walked away, leaving Paul in the lurch. Besides abandoning him physically, Demas forsook Paul emotionally and spiritually.

How did this once-faithful friend, a man whom Paul trusted, degenerate into a deserter? No one knows for sure how this happened, but William Barclay indicates that it was probably a process, not an overnight phenomenon.

> There are three mentions of [Demas] in Paul's letters; and it may well be that they have in them the story of a tragedy. (i) In Philemon 24 he is listed amongst a group of men whom Paul calls his fellow-labourers. (ii) In Colossians 4:14 he is mentioned without any comment at all. (iii) Here he has forsaken Paul because he loved this present world. First, Demas the fellow-labourer, then, just Demas, and, finally, Demas the deserter who loved the world. Here is the history of a spiritual degeneration. Bit by bit the fellow-labourer has become the deserter; the title of honour has become the name of shame.[6]

Even though it took time, Demas eventually walked away when Paul needed him. And Paul was now alone in a dark dungeon cell awaiting execution. But the apostle mentions someone else who

---

5. Craig S. Keener, *The IVP Bible Background Commentary: New Testament* (Downers Grove, Ill.: InterVarsity Press, 1993), p. 623.

6. William Barclay, *The Letters to Timothy, Titus, and Philemon*, rev. ed., The Daily Study Bible Series (Philadelphia, Pa.: Westminster Press, 1975), pp. 212–13.

did him harm. His incarceration might have been a direct result of this other man's aggressive efforts.

Alexander

In Paul's words, "Alexander the coppersmith did me much harm" (v. 14). It's likely that he fingered Paul just as the emperor was looking for Christians to single out and persecute. Paul's imprisonment may very well have resulted from Alexander's efforts. But Alexander wasn't satisfied with merely hurting one man. He also vigorously opposed the gospel (v. 15). Both the man and the message were the targets of his assault.

Handling Opposition

David's and Paul's experiences teach us that we cannot expect to make an impact for Christ without encountering opposition. Whether it's the defection of a Demas or the direct assaults of a King Saul or an Alexander, opposition will come in some form. So we must be spiritually and emotionally ready to confront it. But how? What should we do? If we look closely at how David and Paul responded, we can pick up two important principles about handling opposition.

Don't Retaliate

As Saul pursued him through the wilderness, David had two opportunities to kill him. Once, when Saul ducked into a cave where David was hiding, he resisted temptation and merely cut off the edge of the king's robe (see 1 Sam. 24). Later, as Saul slept, David sneaked into his camp and stole Saul's own spear and water jug, again refusing to kill God's anointed (see chap. 26). David, although anointed to be the next king himself, still treated his enemy with grace. He refused to take revenge.

Paul also refrained from retaliation. Look at what he said about Alexander: "The Lord will repay him according to his deeds" (2 Tim. 4:14). Paul was not going to spend one ounce of energy contemplating revenge. Just like David, he knew God would take care of his opponents, and he trusted in that fact. Referring to all those who abandoned him, he said, "May it not be counted against them" (v. 16). Paul was on death row, remember. And he forgave them! What an incredible expression of grace.

Look to the Lord in Faith

David and Paul were able to treat their enemies with grace because they looked to the Lord in faith. They didn't become paralyzed with fear and anxiety. They didn't waste their time involving themselves in scuffles that belonged to the Lord. They didn't give in to the temptation to save their egos or to put their opponents in their places. The glory of God's name took priority over their pride.

We know that, as Saul sought to kill him, David trusted God for protection. He told Saul,

> "The Lord therefore be judge and decide between you and me; and may He see and plead my cause and deliver me from your hand." (1 Sam. 24:15)

Paul did the same thing:

> The Lord will rescue me from every evil deed, and will bring me safely to His heavenly kingdom; to Him be the glory forever and ever. Amen. (2 Tim. 4:18)

Both David and Paul transcended their opposition through a victorious faith that committed their present and future into God's hands. And we can do the same, knowing that the Lord is not only *with* us always, but is always *for* us too (see Matt. 28:20; Rom. 8:31–39).

Conclusion

Have you ever been deserted by a Demas? Has a Saul or an Alexander attacked you? You're not alone. Paul and David have been there—and so has Jesus. When you face opposition for the sake of the gospel, God is on your side. Paul said it beautifully in Romans 8:31: "If God is for us, who is against us?" The implied answer is: Absolutely no one.

However large or small, passive or aggressive the opposition that comes your way, never forget who stands with you. David and Paul are watching. And Jesus is standing by your side. Hold on to that, and know that through it all, He's holding onto you.

 *Living Insights*

Let's bring the principles David and Paul have shown us up close to our lives. Even if you're not experiencing opposition at the moment, you can still prepare yourself. And if you are facing it right now, these principles will strengthen your resolve to respond God's way.

First, *don't retaliate*. Your first step is to respond to them as God would, which means treating your enemies with grace. To accomplish this, remember your own sin. God had to forgive you, and He wants to do the same with the person who's troubling you. Instead of viewing opposition as a trial, see it as an opportunity in which God may use you to work in their lives. What can you do to lead them to God's forgiveness?

_____

_____

_____

_____

Second, *look to God in faith*. Are you afraid that your enemy will strike again when you lower your guard? Here are a few passages you might find encouraging as you allow God to be your protector. Write out whatever God speaks to you through them.

Psalm 46 _____

_____

_____

Isaiah 43:1–7_____

_____

_____

Romans 8:35–39_____

_____

_____

Chapter 6

HISTORIC MARKER

Joshua 4:1–9; Deuteronomy 6:4–13, 24

What a memorable journey this has been!

We started at the "narrow bridge" and found the way to heaven —through faith in Jesus Christ alone. Not long after crossing the bridge, we encountered a "dangerous curve," realizing our sinful nature wouldn't go away quietly. Then we pulled into God's "roadside park" for some much-needed rest from life in the fast lane. Back on the road again, we learned to "drive friendly" by allowing other Christians their freedom in Christ. Next, at the "railroad crossing," we learned to face opposition. A memorable trip all right. And, hopefully, a helpful one as well. But there's one more signpost up ahead: the historic marker.

The concept of historic markers dates back to the ancient world. Most civilizations leave behind monuments—reminders of their greatness to subsequent generations. The Babylonians built their Hanging Gardens, and the Athenians erected the Acropolis. The ancient Spartans chose to build a different kind of historic marker. They built monuments, not out of stone, but out of stories, immortalizing their warriors through tales of heroism.

One of the most intriguing monuments ever built, however, was not devoted to heroic men but to a heroic God. And the monument itself took a lowly form—a simple pile of muddy rocks pulled from the Jordan River. But what a monument! While the structure was crude, the rocks spoke volumes about the greatest empire ever assembled—the people of God. Unlike other monuments, however, it testified to its people's weakness instead of their might. This historic marker reminded Israel of their dependance on Yahweh. Like a King born in a manger, the rock pile monument required its admirers to look beyond the surface to find its true significance.

Stones of Remembrance

The true significance of that pile of rocks is the simple message of faith in God and His provision. And that message, along with the rest of God's Word, will last forever (see Isa. 40:8).

How did that pile of rocks come to be? It's one of God's greatest stories. Joshua and the next generation of Israelites stood poised on the brink of the Promised Land. All that stood between them was the rush of the Jordan River, swollen with the melting of Mount Hermon's winter snows. As a sign that He was just as much with them as He was with their parents, God parted the river's waters— as He had parted the Red Sea some forty years earlier—and the people walked across on dry land.

Joshua then followed God's blueprint for building an everlasting memorial.

> Joshua called the twelve men whom he had appointed from the sons of Israel, one man from each tribe; and Joshua said to them, "Cross again to the ark of the Lord your God into the middle of the Jordan, and each of you take up a stone on his shoulder, according to the number of the tribes of the sons of Israel. Let this be a sign among you, so that when your children ask later, saying, 'What do these stones mean to you?' then you shall say to them, 'Because the waters of the Jordan were cut off before the ark of the covenant of the Lord; when it crossed the Jordan, the waters of the Jordan were cut off.' So these stones shall become a memorial to the sons of Israel forever."
>
> Thus the sons of Israel did as Joshua commanded. (Josh. 4:4–8a)

God didn't command the Hebrews to stack those stones so they could learn about rocks. He did it so they would remember the Rock, God Himself, and His steadfast faithfulness to His people.

And so it is with us. From this story we can learn at least three things.

First, *God wants us to go to the trouble of establishing historic markers.* God commands and blesses the establishing of historic markers to Him throughout Scripture. The pattern emerges when God established the Passover as a memorial of the Exodus (Exod. 12:23–28). That pattern is sustained in such things as the Feast of Unleavened Bread (13:3–10), the rock pile at the Jordan, and Samuel's laying down of the Ebenezer stone (1 Sam. 7:12). And what more vivid monument to God's grace than the Lord's Supper (1 Cor. 11:23–26).

Clearly, God wants us to make the effort of establishing monuments. Have you thought about doing this in your family? Your historic markers need not be stones, though they can be. They could be plaques written by you and your children. They could be etchings or even journals that record what God has done for you, that preserve a snapshot of His grace for your children and grandchildren to see. God wants us to go to the trouble so that future generations will remember and be encouraged.

Second, *God cares about our remembering Him and what He has done.* Historic markers themselves are not nearly as important as the people or events they commemorate. When we consider Noah, do we first think of the altar he built after the flood? Of course not; we remember God's deliverance. What about Abraham when he left Ur for the Promised Land? Do we think of the altar he established there or God's faithful leading? The same could be said of many other biblical characters. In this way, historic markers are exalted memory aids because they point to something more significant than themselves. They point to God Himself.

God doesn't want us to ever forget what He has done or who He is. The word *remember,* in fact, occurs more than 160 times in Scripture. And the words of the psalmists provide a timeless challenge for us: "Remember His wonders which He has done, His marvels and the judgments uttered by His mouth. . . . Bless the Lord, O my soul, And forget none of His benefits" (Ps. 105:5; 103:2).

And last, *God cares just as much that our children remember Him and what He has done.* If we fail to establish markers commemorating what the Lord has done, our children may never know His deeds. If the only instruction they receive comes from society, they will most assuredly forget God. So we must erect markers for our children in places they will certainly see—and home receives the most traffic. We can't depend on the church to resurrect what a home never brought to life. No, it's home where life makes up its mind and where life establishes its etchings.

Three Essentials for Passing on Your Faith

Before Joshua and the Israelites had prepared to cross the Jordan, Moses had taken the time to prepare them for their new lives. How? By reminding them of God's Law and God's love. By passing on the faith. From Moses' words to that young generation in Deuteronomy 6, we can learn how to pass on our faith to the generation after us, how to prepare our children to stand strong in God after we're gone.

Love God

Moses said to the people,

> "You shall love the Lord your God with all your
> heart and with all your soul and with all your might."
> (Deut. 6:5)

This is a difficult command in any society, especially an idola-
trous one—one where different gods and different beliefs bombard
both parents' and children's minds. To defend against the onslaught
of false faiths, we need to ground our children in the truth, repeating
over and over that we're to love the one true God. And we're to love
Him with all our hearts. Because God is after a love that goes below
the surface. He wants the deepest part of us—our hearts (v. 6). So
before anything else, we must cultivate the habit of loving God
deeply.

Teach Your Children

Not only must we authentically love God ourselves, but we
must actively teach our children to love Him as well. Notice verse
7a: "You shall teach [God's words] diligently to your sons." *Diligently*
in Hebrew is a graphic term. Its root word means "to sharpen,"
indicating incisive teaching. This tells us that our instruction needs
to be direct and firm, intentional and to the point.

In teaching our children, however, wisdom is just as important
as diligence. If we instruct them too forcibly or if we're insensitive
to good timing, they may develop a distaste for God instead of a
love for Him. It's hard for anyone, especially hungry kids, to sit at
the dinner table and listen to an extended Bible reading or a long
prayer as the aromas from fresh bread and warm stew waft into their
noses. We should make every effort to make learning God's Word
palatable and timely, if not fun and exciting.

It's also important to make our teaching natural, not forced.
Moses told the people,

> "[You] shall talk of them when you sit in your house
> and when you walk by the way and when you lie
> down and when you rise up." (v. 7b)

Spiritual lessons come in the course of daily life: when we're
driving, when we're walking, when we're eating, when we're shopping or doing laundry or waking up our children or putting them

to bed. Teaching is much more effective when it's done naturally and easily rather than formally or forcefully. This is how we can fashion a home for God's glory (v. 9).

Don't Forget

Moses next issued a warning to the Israelites:

> "It shall come about when the Lord your God brings you into the land which He swore to your fathers, Abraham, Isaac and Jacob, to give you, great and splendid cities which you did not build, and houses full of all good things which you did not fill, . . . and you eat and are satisfied, *then watch yourself, that you do not forget the Lord* who brought you from the land of Egypt, out of the house of slavery." (vv. 10–12, emphasis added)

Parents, when your children are born into a Christian family, be aware of how easy it is for them to take "faith" for granted. They've never known what life outside of Christ is like, how empty it is and how precious God's grace is. So tell them about your life before Christ came into it, tell them about your salvation, and help them see the wonder of God's gift. Don't let your heritage of "spiritual affluence" become "spiritual impoverishment" for your kids. Help them remember God.

One way to keep them mindful of the Lord is to instill a healthy fear of Him, which means having an awesome respect for His power and position. Moses said, "You shall fear only the Lord your God; and you shall worship Him and swear by His name" (v. 13). Notice the relationship in the verse between fearing God and being faithful to Him. If we respect His strength, we'll be faithful to Him in worship and in our daily lives.

As soon as the Israelites would enter the land, they would be surrounded by Canaanites. So they needed a reminder to fear only the one true God. If they did, they would stand a better chance of being faithful to Him and would avoid becoming trapped in a Canaanite mentality. As Moses told them,

> "So the Lord commanded us to observe all these statutes, to fear the Lord our God for our good always and for our survival, as it is today." (v. 24)

When we love God wholeheartedly and teach our children to do the same, we protect their faith from becoming diluted or polluted by the society that surrounds them. Remembering and fearing God helps them maintain their faithfulness to Him.

Four Theological Markers to Erect

Now that we know what it takes to pass on our faith, which historic markers should we concentrate on building for the generations after us? Here are four suggestions.

God Is Love

First John 4:8 tells us that "God is love." We can establish a monument to love in our homes by loving others the way God loves them. Living in love will prevent a home from being filled with resentment, unforgiveness, grudges, selfishness, prejudice, and retaliation. And our young people will learn to apply God's love in the midst of conflict if they see their parents doing that. We establish a monument to God's love when our children see it in us and receive it from us.

God Is Holy

"Holy, Holy, Holy, is the Lord of hosts," the prophet recorded, declaring God's triune holiness (Isa. 6:3). And as Peter tells us, this has certain implications for us: "Like the Holy One who called you, be holy yourselves" (1 Pet. 1:15). "Holy" essentially means "set apart." In practical terms, that means we should live our lives with the understanding that we are God's people, created to have a relationship with Him and to do His work. One of the most obvious outworkings of holiness is moral purity. When our children see us enjoying a relationship with God and living a pure life, they see holiness. Just as with love, displaying it is the best way to pass it on.

God Is Faithful

As Jeremiah wrote,

The Lord's lovingkindnesses indeed never cease,
For His compassions never fail.
They are new every morning;
Great is Your faithfulness. (Lam. 3:22–23)

God never changes (see Heb. 13:8). No matter how our circumstances evolve or devolve. No matter how much our society

42

degenerates. God is always the same, and He will always be faithful to us. As His children, we try to reciprocate that faithfulness. Often, it means waiting on Him, trusting Him, and that can be difficult in a society that has taught us to demand instant gratification. If our children see us display loyalty and patience in seeking His will, they stand a good chance of avoiding the pitfalls of anxiety and worry and will probably become faithful followers themselves.

God Is Sovereign

God is sovereign over both human events and creation (see Dan. 4:34–35; Ps. 139:1–12). Ultimately, this means that He is powerfully in control of everything. When we truly come to terms with this, we'll no longer feel compelled to take charge in the midst of confusing events or to resist them.

How do we establish this marker? Life provides many teachable moments in which we can communicate God's sovereignty to our children. When Grandma dies, we can provide comfort by saying, "Honey, Grandma's with Jesus now, and we'll see her again some day." When our political candidates lose, we can say, "God is still on the throne," instead of, "That man will ruin our country." As St. Augustine once summed up, "We count on God's mercy for our past mistakes, God's love for our present needs, and God's sovereignty for the future."[1] Let's teach our children that, with God in control, they can look to the future with joy.

Conclusion

Historic markers are memory aids and teaching tools for reminding us—and our children—what God has done. He wants us to build them so that we will remember Him and, most importantly, so that our children will know Him and His ways.

What will our spiritual legacy be? Passing on our faith to our children can be a beautiful highlight of a journey well traveled, of a life well lived. Yes, we must perfect the other signposts first— crossing the narrow bridge, navigating the dangerous curves, resting at the roadside park, driving friendly, and passing the railroad crossing. But if we do them well and model an authentic faith to our children, our historic marker will be a God-honoring one.

1. Attributed to St. Augustine, source unknown.

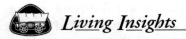 *Living Insights*

American poet Carl Sandburg described the future of all great societies in his poem "Four Preludes on Playthings of the Wind."

"The past is a bucket of ashes."

1

The woman named Tomorrow
sits with a hairpin in her teeth
and takes her time
and does her hair the way she wants it
and fastens at last the last braid and coil
and puts the hairpin where it belongs
and turns and drawls: Well, what of it?
My grandmother, Yesterday, is gone.
What of it? Let the dead be dead.

2

The doors were cedar
and the panels strips of gold
and the girls were golden girls
and the panels read and the girls chanted:
        We are the greatest city,
        the greatest nation:
        nothing like us ever was.
The doors are twisted on broken hinges.
Sheets of rain swish through on the wind
        where the golden girls ran and the panels read:
        We are the greatest city,
        the greatest nation,
        nothing like us ever was.

3

It has happened before.
Strong men put up a city and got
        a nation together,
And paid singers to sing and women
        to warble: We are the greatest city,
            the greatest nation,
            nothing like us ever was.

And while the singers sang

and the strong men listened
and paid the singers well
and felt good about it all,
    there were rats and lizards who listened
    . . . and the only listeners left now
    . . . are . . . the rats . . . and the lizards.

And there are black crows
crying, "Caw, caw,"
bringing mud and sticks
building a nest
over the words carved
on the doors where the panels were cedar
and the strips on the panels were gold
and the golden girls came singing:
    We are the greatest city,
    the greatest nation:
    nothing like us ever was.

The only singers now are crows crying, "Caw, caw,"
And the sheets of rain whine in the wind and doorways.
And the only listeners now are . . . the rats . . . and the lizards.

4

The feet of the rats
scribble on the doorsills;
the hieroglyphs of the rat footprints
chatter the pedigree of the rats
and babble of the blood
and gabble of the breed
of the grandfathers and the great-grandfathers
of the rats.

And the wind shifts
and the dust on the doorsill shifts
and even the writing of the rat footprints
tells us nothing, nothing at all
about the greatest city, the greatest nation
where the strong men listened
and the women warbled: Nothing like us ever was.[2]

2. "Four Preludes on Playthings of the Wind" from *Smoke and Steel* by Carl Sandburg, copyright 1920 by Harcourt Brace and Company and renewed 1948 by Carl Sandburg, reprinted by permission of the publisher.

What will we leave our children and grandchildren and great-grandchildren? Are we building monuments to ourselves, monuments that will crumble in time, or lasting monuments to God?

Take a few moments to consider some practical ways you can pass on your faith and your God to your descendants. Using the four monuments we've suggested, list ways you can model those characteristics to your children.

God is love: _____

_____

_____

_____

God is holy: _____

_____

_____

_____

God is faithful: _____

_____

_____

_____

God is sovereign: _____

_____

_____

_____

_____

BOOKS FOR
PROBING FURTHER

Interest levels vary greatly among travelers. Some speed along the freeway with no concern for the people or places they pass. Others become great enthusiasts who write whole books on just one place or one stretch of highway. This study guide has attempted to introduce you to the wonderful scenes that lie along the road for Christians who are willing to pay closer attention. If the guide has sparked a deeper interest in you, the following books will help you delve deeper into the Christian topography.

Busséll, Harold L. *Lord, I Can Resist Anything but Temptation.* Grand Rapids, Mich.: Zondervan Publishing House, Pyranee Books, 1985.

Chapman, Steve and Annie, with Maureen Rank. *Gifts Your Kids Can't Break.* Minneapolis, Minn.: Bethany House Publishers, 1991.

Dawn, Marva J. *Keeping the Sabbath Wholly: Ceasing, Resting, Embracing, Feasting.* Grand Rapids, Mich.: William B. Eerdmans Publishing Co., 1989.

Fenton, Horace L., Jr. *When Christians Clash: How to Prevent and Resolve the Pain of Conflict.* Downers Grove, Ill.: InterVarsity Press, 1987.

Jenkins, Jerry B. *Twelve Things I Want My Kids to Remember Forever.* Chicago, Ill.: Moody Press, 1991.

Kincaid, Jorie. *The Power of Modeling.* Colorado Springs, Colo.: NavPress, 1989.

Lutzer, Erwin W. *How to Say No to a Stubborn Habit.* Wheaton, Ill.: Scripture Press Publications, Victor Books, 1979.

McDowell, Josh. *More Than a Carpenter.* Wheaton, Ill.: Tyndale House Publishers, Living Books, 1977.

Malony, H. Newton. *When Getting Along Seems Impossible.* Old Tappan, N.J.: Fleming H. Revell Co., 1989.

Morison, Frank. *Who Moved the Stone?* 1930. Reprint, Grand Rapids, Mich.: Zondervan Publishing House, Lamplighter Books, 1958.

Some of the books listed may be out of print and available only through a library. For those currently available, please contact your local Christian bookstore. Books by Charles R. Swindoll may be obtained through Insight for Living, as well as some books by other authors. Just call the IFL office that serves you.

NOTES

NOTES

ORDERING INFORMATION

SIGNPOSTS ALONG LIFE'S JOURNEY

If you would like to order additional study guides, purchase the cassette series that accompanies this guide, or request our product catalogs, please contact the office that serves you.

United States and International Locations:

Insight for Living
Post Office Box 69000
Anaheim, CA 92817-0900
1-800-772-8888, 24 hours a day, 7 days a week
(714) 575-5000, 8:00 A.M. to 4:30 P.M., Pacific time, Monday
to Friday

Canada:

Insight for Living Ministries
Post Office Box 2510
Vancouver, BC, Canada V6B 3W7
1-800-663-7639, 24 hours a day, 7 days a week

Australia:

Insight for Living, Inc.
General Post Office Box 2823 EE
Melbourne, VIC 3001, Australia
(03) 9877-4277, 8:30 A.M. to 5:00 P.M., Monday to Friday

World Wide Web:

www.insight.org

Study Guide Subscription Program

Study guide subscriptions are available. Please call or write the office nearest you to find out how you can receive our study guides on a regular basis.